the things we
outgrew

Aubrey McFadden

Presentation by *BookLeaf Publishing*

Web: www.bookleafpub.com

E-mail: info@bookleafpub.com

ISBN: 978-93-95755-45-0

First edition 2022

Ms. McBryan

*Thank you for believing in me, even when I
didn't believe in myself.*

Rubble

The flowers will bloom and they will die
Then they will bloom again

You can not build on a broken wall

Packing Tape

She's leaving soon
Packing and going soon
Box by box
Do you think she's scared?
That girl in the mirror

Come Back

I forgot about today
And yesterday too.
I don't know where there going but I leave soon
I thought I'd have more time, that maybe it was
just a twisted dream, but everything is moving
so quickly and I can't breathe.

Can you hold me again?

Like you did years ago?

I know I hardly see you and we don't talk
anymore
But I always remember that day, and the way the
time flowed, we danced around the living room
to the TVs glow.
It's just me now I feel alone
One of these days, I promise, I'll find a home

Pinkie Promise

Why did you lie to me all those years ago?
I look back on those days and I know.
We were never something special but you
treated it that way
You would laugh at my jokes and I would ask
you to stay.

I don't know you now, I know we both changed
but I feel like I'm learning new things every day

Whose heart did you give me?

I still have it here but, we're empty now in a way
I don't understand.
If I give it back will you look me in the eyes?
and know me like you swore you did.

Misshapen

5

I'm scared that I don't belong here anymore
I put my heart in these walls
I think I left my happiness at your house
Is my laughter still in your car?

I'll bury my soul in the ground and come back
for it later

Pieces

I want to be everything I'm not
I want to save the parts you like
I don't know who I am on my own

I'll try to be something you could love

Cheap Plastic

The world around me is crumbling down
I'll save what I can and live my life like some
cheap knock off

Bonfire

The warmth of the fire
The warmth of the drink
I sit there and I think,

I hope you feel the joy I do
You are all I want to be

Stop

Can I stay here in this empty mind?
No standards, no time
My life is so full when in with you
This is all I want to be

Long Road

It's foggy up ahead
I can't see that far
I'm afraid to take another step
and lose my way home

Chrysalis

I will bury my burdens in my childhood home
Hold my hopes tightly so they don't slip through
my fingers
I've lost myself
Become something new

Young & Old

I want to walk these halls again
Standing in the doorway to talk
I want to see you again
Running across the street holding your hand
I want to be young again
Sitting side by side with no plan

Childhood Dreams

I heard their laughter
I wanted to be loved

I saw their painted smiles
I wanted to be beautiful

I listened to their praise
I wanted to be smart

I look at their tear stained face
I want to be happy

Remember

I want to see you before I go
Before I forget who we are
I want to see you before I change
into something you don't recognize

Goodbye

I'll put my head on your shoulder
Forget my fears
I'll hold you in my arms
Pray that time stands still

New Moon

It's dark outside
I can't close my eyes

Will you hold my hand again?
I don't know how to be alone

Owner's Manual

I'll see you again
It will all be okay
We will figure this world out
One of these days

Home

If I cry on your shoulder
you won't tell, right?
If I hold onto you a bit tight
Is it okay if I never want to leave?